Sensuality.

Poems

Mary K Gowdy

CONTENTS

Shades of Blood

When I hear a song or read another's
words, I dip into their heads—their faces,
their voices shadowed in mine as I feel the
blood of the bed of the lover of the
            darling Annabel Lee,

the arousing knife of woman's fury,
the dissonance of an opheliac
running in me. You say it shows me something
I haven't felt, but by how it springs from
            deep within my body

to the surface, its shade must rest in me.
Might all the shades lie inside and will surge
forward if I open my veins? And how far
into the darkest crypt of a person's
            mind and soul should I creep?

But I must release this blood—both the bleak
and the acceptable psyches—to live.
The opheliac drenches me in her soul's
sensation, determining every stroke
            to seem rawer than the

personas we dress us in normally.
Is this creation farther from the truth?
Then how can it drill to people's centers by
writing around it in circles, 'less we
          enhance the colors' hues

with our shades? As it becomes my turn to
give life through death—to resurrect the both
of us for but a moment—what will you see
when you open my pages to dip your
          fingers into my blood?

Pluvia Purgans

She is goddess of rain, an elegant dancing
muse with footsteps like raindrops pattering, passing
dripping days in her peaceful trances of movement,
leaving life for fancy and finally relaxing.

Shadow Puppets

Why do hands on a piano look so
elegant? Is it how the fingers curve
and move into shapes like making shadow
puppets? No, it's because they truly serve
the beauty that lies within their maestro,
transforming the face that you had known first.
The allure of birds on the wall is made
in what you may glimpse within the dim shapes.

A Ladder of Notes

The soft guitar drained the moment of all but
the crawl of notes up the ladder of its strings.
In night, the car drove; inside, my time was stopped.
The soft guitar drained the moment of all but
the darkness that dragged me inward and then cupped
the light so blue below of the city's ring.
The soft guitar drained the moment of all but
the crawl of notes up the ladder of its strings.

A Bonfire

Sound, light, time—
beauty and power
lie in their evanescence.
The fire spun like a dancing woman's skirt,
gliding up on the skin of the wind
to pass away to dust that falls
to grow the grass to die again.

Untitled

I wish I was a
particle of your sweat so I
could drip down your brow, ooze
over your cheek, and
mingle with your laborious
scent.

Sinking

As you lean in, I am subdued, inhaling
fluttery breaths down my throat. I want to rest
into you, blend into your body, losing
myself in your scent.

Entranced, numbing fantasies of you in me
come to mind as smoothly as slumber. Never
straying, I wonder to you, wanting you here,
resigned to my path.

On sand, clingy tar in my toes, I sink in
soothing surrender to your essence, venom
crawling up my nose to my mind's eye, cloying,
drowning me.

Dancing the "Shadowmaker"

The dancers tiptoe onto the
stage, their toes lightly rippling a lake's
surface, sending out sound waves, prickly
and playful, tiny drops bound to crescendo into
booms. They are alluring and indulgent as
they dance around the pointe of their tragedy.
Squirming in his tight embrace, she longs to
loosen and fly over so wide a stage. But,
strong from the stance of his feet to the
vice of his hands, he pulls her through
the measures to tiptoe around him till
her legs buckle. As she slips, he
clutches her desperately.
She has almost gone away when he
jerks
her back to the old movement,
but damage has drummed its discord.
They strain for their own ends,
fastened by the knot
of their fingers. Their feet beat
relentlessly before blooming
into a cry of vigorous
yet beguiling motions.
She's a breath,
itching to utter
a note,
a word.
Snatching her
hair, he forces her down and
drags her as she roots herself to
the floor. She breaks out

and flees, but
with each
step,
uncertainty
pounds her to her knees.
She looks behind, and he
with loving fire
half-carries her off
-stage.
The music revs away, filled with
chugging anxiety, climaxing
into cries that twist and
seize like shadows on the
walls. In its wake,
the thread tightens
wanting to sing but is strangled
into a screech by Dread,
who swallows it in Its quiet.
The notes sway up and down
like
warm breaths, in and out,
supported
by a heartbeat, forceful then
delicate—
a yanking
of notes,
a crash of cymbals
across a face.

All is quiet.
Give a little, take a little,
a lesson in
seduction and horror.

The breath explodes
into voice
and cannot be quieted. Like bile,
it burns the body in its
tearing upward trajectory.
For once built up,
it must break out. She careens
in frenzied pirouettes to
grace every crevice with her
essence. Each footfall speeds up
the tempo with a chime.
On the edge,
he watches her
with the scars of someone
so in love he can't see day.
As she slows, her feet patter their
way back to him.
She's a lover's heartbeat,
anxious,
hopeful.
All of her draws to him,
heels rising to take a new step,
as his hands fall over her to caress
her face,
over her jaw,
down to her neck.

All is silent
in anticipation of
that first pitch—
Screams retch through
silence, every innard
power turned inside out

of her strangled throat in a
grotesque aria till nothing is left
but the wick of her candle.
Her knees fall like drumbeats, followed
by her hands,
one, two, three, four.
He snakes his arm down
her waist and pulls her into
the light steps of before, now his
doll to be led though heavy in his
embrace.
Just as her feet return to the dance,
she flickers back to life with a wrench
of her arm's bow.
Twice, she almost escapes but
is snatched back by his strength.
When she is crawling,
she kicks back,
not looking
. . .and he falls.

Her Gaze

A candle among many, lighting, lilting flames,
from one to another, each signaling the beginning.
Blowing dust from the wall, I paint the lines,

tentative sketches like the first steps, climbing
up hills, the burning fields as I remember:
the sounds, the chants as we draft down the damning

doom of our rebellion. Wreck our tormentors,
the lavish ones in their lone ebony tower.
We march with all our great onslaught's splendor.

I, one soldier among many, stride through the despair
of the broken buildings' torn-up streets. I slip on
their blood pouring from their guts to devour

the city in a slick red rain. Once daylight is gone,
we, breaking battle, lay our tired bodies down,
but always wary, always anxious. Envisioning

her, I rewind: the shower window, rivulets are rounding
down streets through the sultry steam,
blinding us to everything but longing announced

by the paths fingers follow down the skin. Between
her lips, a plea for me to come back, she, trembling—
a trembling in the blood-soaked ground, teeming

with us fighters once more. Taking down the emblem.
Break the gates. Now the door, swinging out with a creak—
splinters slice skin, bricks mutilate men at random.

Numb and bleeding, I stumble to my feet.
Everywhere people are spilled on the ground
like cards decked down on the floor. "Retreat!"

someone coughs. Airships drowning it, pound-pound,
pass the city, to the lake, over the haven. Another explosion,
breaking her, me, my word. I can't go back-can't rewind.

Can't rewind—only remember—paint with repeating motions
the impression, stroking the valleys and the troughs.
Last touch. Depict the cruelty done in those moments.

She, lying down with a toe dipped lazily in the slosh
of the old lake, her heel a haven. Paths wound up her shins
and across one cheek, down her back's hollow, and up off

to the city of her shoulders, knives of the buildings singed
through her spine. The army up her neck approaching
the tower of her hair, the deadly mystery entrenched.

Finished, I leave, blowing out the flames.
Her gaze demands remembrance for the slain.

The Primordial

I want–
I-I want–
I want. . .

You.

I don't want to kiss you.
I don't want to date you.
I don't want to fuck you.
I don't want to __.

My want
is more primal than 'to __'.
It evolved in what came before
the first movement of life.

How can you satisfy a want
that penetrates deeper than sex,
that is unchained by language,
that is older than action?

Victoria's Secret

I

Once, a man did look at me, so
charmed with what he saw, he forgot
his gaze—a tad dramatic, I know
—but that which he made to me,
that I perceived,
was then for me reality.

Then, he did forget his gaze,
and I desired not his love but
for him to stare at me the same
—if only for one chime.
Ever since I have lusted to lasso a
pair of eyes to call them mine.

II

I'd skip through the halls,
yodeling off-pitch, if it'd cause
you to look at me and fill the space
of that chime.
But what I want is to handcuff you
to a chair and dance for you naked,
so you, frustrated at your manual
amputation, are forced to caress me
with those eyes.

But I know that my pleasure is
not birthed from you, but from me
for Victoria's Secret lies
in my sexuality.
It was when I was able to gaze
at myself that I began to want not
others but others to want me,
the secret request, in the world
unspoken, Eve's taboo want to
indulge in a selfish
sensuality:

to inhabit the pupil
of your eye.

The Voices of a Violin

Turn up the speaker and dream of sluggish summer
days when you'd sit outside to
sweat.

Of how you'd complain and jump into the water
before hands could push you,
teasing hands that would ruthlessly
splash you
but then trace the rivulets of your back so
lightly you'd fear they had
evaporated.

Of how restful it was to reduce the world
to damp grass, purple sunsets,
laughs, and a breathy voice at your
neck.

Of how that voice and its breath would get under your skin,
its coverings cast aside and beautiful in its
nakedness, refined
down to a pinprick
to breach the
sky of your consciousness
before falling
to the base of your being,
as the sun must be swallowed
by the
horizon.

Of how in that last flash before darkness,
your voice escaped to accompany it.
Your twisting timbres convulsed
the seconds away
between crafted song and sweaty moans
to scrape
the bottom of Sound's bowl,
squeezing out every last drop
to drink
to make
that summer's sun
last.

Of how Time inevitably bended
those seconds agonizingly slow
yet ephemeral,
and the cries
grow to their full ecstasy
just as they sink further
into the haze of
memory.

Dancing to "Bedroom Hymns"

The shadows move close to the ground,
right, left, slide,
three claps
that crackle their batons with sparks,
breaking open to birth fire.

Right, left, slides the light
across contours of bodies
to engrave the skin
gold and black.

Another clap as the batons
collide to move from left hand to
right, and falls into their circle of fire
the one with the fire within,
the slap of her palms and knees muted
by the lush grass.

She twists, crouched to the ground
like the dancers around her, and
rakes her hands and knees against every
blade of grass and dust of dirt
to sanctify it.

She slowly rises, stretching her limbs
till the muscles release to make her skin warm
with the nearness of her blood,
her movements as elegant as her braided hair.

She sees him watching from outside
the circle of flames, but when she runs
to him, the dancers whirl around,
seizing her in their current of bodies
and melodious bellow, and
push her back
into the middle of their boundary.

She lies on her back and
digs her fingers into the soil,
imagining drinking in his life like a
root with water—
as pleasurable in the dousing
as in her burning.

Glancing slightly over her shoulder at him,
she runs her finger over the lips of her smile,
and dances out her frustration
in the tearing of her braid and
the sensuality of her being,
teasing herself just as much as him.

He treads the boundary as he watches.
Sparks are the children of his feet,
and her self-caresses his tightening chains.

Again, she fights to reach him,
and again, the dancers speed up
to hold her back.
Her hair falls free around her waist,
its tresses the ghost of touches.

But then,
damp palms clutch her hips,
pressing down in the slide up her stomach.
She collapses against him, back to chest,
and covers his hands with hers
to grasp her breasts and
cup her neck
as she yells to make physical
the sound of her sensation.

She faces him,
raking her fingers through the
hair of his chest and the sweat of his skin
to pull him to her, as her voice
rises to the clarity of light
and then rests in the blood of her mouth.

He lifts her hand to slide his fingers
in the space between hers,
left with right,
just as the dancers
dunk them into their frenzied stream,
swinging them right, left,
but they can't—won't—break
the flesh of their hand.

As their bodies and flames blur
so do their voices—
the cries, the bellows,
the laughs, the screams—
all partials
building over the fundamental that is
their voice.

Winding down,
the dancers depart from the two—
her and him, shaky as they all descend into
stillness.

La Petite Mort

You describe it like electricity,
frame it in a world of technology.
Have I fallen out of time from an era
where the trinity of my libido
      be death, music, and verse?

Now, before you think that I am perverse,
consider poets, the philosophers
of old, and that singer you see on the stage.
All know that ecstasy lies in the will
      to fill oneself and die.

See how she bows her head, closes her eyes
to let the music poison her, drawing
out a spirit so sensual in the depths
of its emotion and will to scrape life
      under its fingernails.

I listen to song to unfurl my sails;
to leave and let that woman stand and sing.
I am gone but rest and feel that her body,
as I have died and been reborn slightly
      changed, is still somewhere mine.

At the brush of skin or sound, I consign
myself to the blood of tone on my lips.
Oh, let its weight drip me to my body's ground
because sex is the filling with it and
        death the losing of it.

You may argue that this doesn't befit
me, but I'll always prefer the groan of
a violin over a synthesizer's
whisper. Give me blood and dirt too filthy
        for your filtered water.

Acknowledgements

First, I'm eternally grateful to my dear friend Thaddeus Cochrane for your support among so many other things. You were the first to read these poems, came up with a badass title when all my suggestions were crap, and helped me realize part of my dream by producing the recordings for *Sensuality*..

Many thanks to the UNT Creative Writing Club, who despite suffering from metrophobia came through to give me useful feedback on this chapbook anyway. Our club meetings are one of the funnest parts of my week.

For my friends who came to my open mic night performances, thank you so much. I don't believe I could've gotten on that stage if ya'll hadn't been there.

Thanks to the literary magazine *Better Than Starbucks* for originally publishing "Shadow Puppets".

I give thanks to my God, who gave me the gift of words that I did nothing to deserve.

And finally, I'd like to thank you, the reader. I'm humbled that you would consider my thoughts chronicled here worthy of your time. I hope you enjoyed reading these poems as much as I enjoyed writing them.

I believe that listening to poetry is an important part of enjoying it. Recordings of all fourteen of *Sensuality.*'s poems are posted on my YouTube Channel
http://www.youtube.com/c/MaryKGowdy

You can listen to them here:
https://www.youtube.com/playlist?list=PLfm-32vidIfAJdJrcJvM9DGw78VBc2qp5

Mary K Gowdy is the poet behind the collections *Sensuality.*, *Where Have We Come From, Where Are We Going*, and *Leftover Thoughts*. Her work has appeared in literary magazines such as *The Anti-Misogyny Club, SpecPoVerse*, and *Sheila-Na Gig* and in the indie anthology *Writing Out Our Twenties*. She also has published two fantasy novels in her epic series *The One and the Other*. When not writing, she enjoys being in nature, listening to music, and convincing her friends that poetry is nothing to be afraid of.

CONTACT ME
www.marykgowdy.com
Instagram @marykgowdy
TikTok @maryk.gowdy

Want more?
If you sign up for my email list, you can get the first 4
chapters of my fantasy novel The One-Sided Coin
FOR FREE
Sign up at www.marykgowdy.com

It is the first in an epic fantasy series that combines prose
and poetry.

THE ONE-SIDED COIN
The One and the Other Volume One

When Monoria's institutionalized for burning her house down--with her family in it--she hopes this means that the voice in her mind isn't real. But a scientist informs her that she's infected with a parasite, an abomination originating from the mystic world. As part of the Secularists, an organization intent on eradicating anything mystical, the scientist promises to kill the parasite.

Monoria allows him to run tests, but as his methods turn questionable, she realizes that he might not have her best interests at heart nor be telling her the whole truth. The parasite is dangerous, but it also might be her only ally. It warns her that the Secularists will do anything to achieve their goal, even harming anyone that gets in their way. As the scientist nears a cure, she must decide who to trust-- the scientist determined to destroy mysticism or the parasite that threatens to consume her soul.